SONGS FOR THE UNSUNG...

Lineberger Memorial Library

SONGS FOR THE UNSUNG...

CECIL RAJENDRA

Poems on unpoetic issues
like war and want,
and refugees

THE
RISK
BOOK
SERIES

World Council of Churches, Geneva

The poems in this volume have been selected from the following anthologies of Cecil Rajendra's poems:

Bones & Feathers (Heinemann Educational Books (Asia) Ltd., 1978)

Refugees and other Despairs (Choice Books Pte. Ltd., 1980)

Hour of Assassins and other Poems (Bogle-L'ouverture Publications Ltd., 1983)

We are grateful to the publishers for giving us permission to reproduce them in this volume.

Illustrations: Emi Gemi
Cover design and lay-out: Michael Dominguez
Back cover photo: Christine Thery
ISBN 2-8254-0785-2
© 1983 World Council of Churches, 150 route de Ferney,
1211 Geneva 20, Switzerland
No. 19 in the Risk book series
Printed in Switzerland

for
Rebecca, Yasunari
&
Shakila

Table of contents

The poet and the poems

Cecil Rajendra is a lawyer by profession. He practises in Penang, Malaysia.

Rajendra is also a poet. He is in fact one of the finest poets writing in Asia today. And one of the most controversial.

That's not surprising. Rajendra is not a disinterested artist. He does not believe in "pure" poetry. He would not have his poems enshrined in the "rightful sanctum sanctorum of culture". He would rather speak out — on war and want, on the politics of poverty and the economics of injustice. As he does, fearlessly and passionately, in the poems included in this volume.

Rajendra describes his poems as his "public statements on the times we live in". In that sense they are like the public statements which bodies like the World Council of Churches make — on Peace and Justice, on Human Rights, on the International Food Disorder and similar issues.

There the resemblance ends, though. They are statements; these are poems.

A reviewer of his recent anthology, *Hour of Assassins*, refers to Rajendra as "one-man pressure-group, committed to awakening people to the social evils that beset his country and the world in general".

That's a risky role for a poet to play, in Asia as elsewhere. But Rajendra is not afraid to take risks. He once wrote: "The artist who is not willing to take risks would be better off selling insurance."

We are grateful to Cecil Rajendra for allowing us to publish this selection of his poems in the Risk Book series.

WCC Publications

FROM "DEVELOPING" TO "DEVELOPED"

*We do not accept development as understood,
interpreted and imposed upon us by dominant groups.
We do not want it as it alienates and disintegrates our
people. It destroys human values so precious to us.*

No Place in the Inn
Published by Urban Rural Mission,
Christian Conference of Asia, p. 111

1. Canto of progress

Vibrations of pile-drivers....
the land shudders from
"developing" to "developed"
everywhere tower-blocks
and condominiums mushroom
to eclipse a lowering sky.
High-rise hotels — more
forbidding than the ramparts
of any colonial fortress —
wall us from our beaches.
i watch marauding bull-
dozers scalp the distant hills.

On radio and televion self-
congratulatory announcements
sandwich the advertisements
we reward the rich
decorate the decorated
swop last year's Merz
for this year's Benz
study the Stock Exchange
check our pocket calculators
applaud the rising G.N.P.
now, isn't our country swell?

Grass and trees and flowers
are in short supply, but
never mind, Ministers assure
us all will be well
in the next Five Year Plan.
In my garden, i notice
the disappearance of butterflies
soon i will have to explain
to my son that a "caterpillar"
is not another genus of tractor!

2. Tourists, transistors or stones

The silent scarecrows
that stood sentinel
over our rice-bowls
have gone ...
And where once
rolling paddy-fields
stretched for miles
now the multinational
electronic factories
roost supreme
Lords of the domain
Messrs Hitachi and Bosch
belch their industrial
filth into our sky
Industrial giants
— like secret agents —
have licences to kill!

Wherever you turn
the story's the same
Development hits you
like a flung knife
I walk down to
the village and find
the local smallholder
who used to supply
our weekly quota
of eggs and vegetable
has been bought over
by a hotel developer
He is now a waiter
in the man's hotel
His daughter
marks time in the
adjoining escort agency.

Sulphur in my heart
I return home
open a newspaper and read
plans are already afoot
to transmogrify my
favourite fishing village
into yet another Mecca
to tantalize the tourists
The fishing stakes are
being ripped out to make
way for a floating casino
bars, massage parlours and all
the paraphernalia of decadence
Meanwhile, the fishermen
will have to buy their fish!

Like every honest citizen
I have no bones
to pick with progress
but if croupiers
and waiters
and foreign investors
take over from
our farmers and fishermen
pray, tell me this
when my son grows up
what will he eat
tourists, transistors or stones?

3. Fisherman's tale

Harvested by trawlers
the field of water
surrounding this bay
has been picked
just about clean
What little there's
left is finished off
by affluence's effluents.

The new coast road
and the latest beach
hotel have backed
the wizened fisherman —
once monarch of all
this strip of land —
up against the hills.

Stealthily, at night
he descends to savour
the memories, to gaze
across the now barren
sea and to cast his
hook and line of tears.

4. Cheap pineapple and sand

And if the soul of this land
is behind the tourist poster
beckoning to sun, sea and sand,
it is equally there in the gutter

where beggars fight off stray
cats for the slop of left-over
dinners, where mice foray
offal cast by itinerant hawkers.

It is there on the peeling
alley walls weeping nicotine-
flecked gobs of phlegm, reeking
putrescent fruit, faeces and urine.

Cheap pineapple and tropical
splendour you now enjoy, dear
traveller, is paid with impossible
lives lived out in unspeakable squalor.

5. When the tourists flew in

The Finance Minister said
    "It will boost the economy
    the dollars will flow in."

The Minister of Interior said
    "It will provide full
    and varied employment
    for the indigenes."

The Ministry of Culture said
    "It will enrich our life ...
    contact with other cultures
    must surely
    improve the texture of living."

The man from the Hilton said
    "We will make you
    a second Paradise;
    for you, it is the dawn
    of a glorious new beginning!"

When the tourists flew in
    our island people
    metamorphosed into
    a grotesque carnival
    — a two-week sideshow

When the tourists flew in
    our men put aside
    their fishing nets
    to become waiters
    our women became whores

When the tourists flew in
    what culture we had
    flew out of the window
    we traded our customs
    for sunglasses and pop
    we turned sacred ceremonies
    into ten-cent peep shows

When the tourists flew in
    local food became scarce
    prices went up
    but our wages stayed low

When the tourists flew in
    we could no longer
    go down to our beaches
    the hotel manager said
    "Natives defile the sea-shore"

When the tourists flew in
    the hunger and the squalor
    were preserved
    as a passing pageant
    for clicking cameras
    — a chic eye-sore!

When the tourists flew in
    we were asked
    to be "side-walk ambassadors"
    to stay smiling and polite
    to always guide
    the "lost" visitor ...
    Hell, if we could only tell them
    where we really want them to go!

6. Kuala Juru — death of a village

Here
intimations of death
hang
heavy in the air
Everywhere
there is the stench
of decay and despair

The river
strangled by
exigencies
of industrialization
is dying ....
and nobody cares

The fish
in the river
poisoned by
progress's vomit
are dying ....
and nobody cares

The birds
that feed on the fish
in the river
poisoned by
progress's excrement
are dying ....
and nobody cares

And so
a once-proud village
sustained
for centuries
by the richness
of this river
dies ....
and nobody cares

To that mammon
DEVELOPMENT
our high-priests
sacrifice
our customs
our culture
our traditions
and environment
and nobody cares

We blind mice
We blind mice
see what we've done
see what we've done
we all ran after
Progress's wife
she cut off our heads
with Development's knife
have you ever seen
such fools in your life
as we blind mice?

7. Consumption

"DO NOT SPIT"
the posters said
"It's disgusting
and it spreads T.B."
Good natives
that we were
we took note
swallowed our spittle
in a National effort
to curb consumption in
that hygiene-conscious
underdeveloped country

Times have changed
No more "Underdeveloped"
we now find ourselves
a "developing" country
"And our task ....
is not to carp
but to catch up!"
The Prime Minister
frames it succinctly

The posters accordingly
keep pace with the age
and the image
They no longer caution
rather cajole
to consumption
of a different kind
Scooters ... Transistors
Egg-beaters ... T.V.

Newly promoted citizens
of an "emergent" society
we may be
but with old
Civil Service obedience
once more we take note
and Buy and Buy and Buy
Our consumption
consumes us irrevocably

It's disgusting
moreover it's expensive
(not like T.B.)
We should have stuck to spitting!

CORRALLED LIKE DUMB CATTLE

The blatant misuse of the concept of national security to justify repression, foreign intervention and spiralling arms budgets is of profound concern... A concept of "common security" of nations must be reinforced by a concept of "people's security". True security for the people demands respect for human rights, including the right to self-determination, as well as social and economic justice for all within every nation, and a political framework that would ensure it.

Gathered for Life
Published by the World Council
of Churches, Geneva, pp. 133-134.

8. Cattle
(for W.S. Rendra)

In windows all over Asia
i see boldly lettered

NO VACANCY

placards going up
on open discussion.
Gates are clanging shut.
To question is subversion.

All is fair game /legislation
in pursuit of prosperity
and security, we're told;
i sniff treachery in the air.

The shutters are coming down
on sanity; lips are pad-
locked; rationality has bolted;
and the people corralled
like dumb cattle are ex-
pected to moo their approval!

9. Maggot memories

My son's cough punches
holes in the night ...
From cobwebs of dreams
i disentangle my eyes
to see if he's alright.

He turns over, clutches
his bolster, slips
into sleep once more.
i have lost that
art of leaping out and
falling back into
the well of dreams
with a child's facility.

There are too many scars.
Too many deaths and losses:
Mahatma Gandhi
Patrice Lumumba
Martin Luther King
Amilcar Cabral
Victor Jara
and now dear Walter Rodney.

The asafoetida memories
of a lifetime
of lives truncated in
full flower
criss-cross the brain
like a shock of maggots
in a gangrenous ulcer ...

and how am i to sleep again?

10. The political prisoner

Under a government which imprisons any unjustly, the
true place for a just man is also a prison — the only
house in a slave state in which a free man can abide
with honour.

Thoreau

Spend no tears
Say no prayers
for the man in
the concrete cage

True, no glimmer
of light beckons
at the end of
the long corridor
of his "future"

Even a whisper
of a trial never
reaches his ear

True, no visitor
calls at his moss-
lined cell to tell
him the time and
integer of year
Only the gaoler
bringing his meagre
ration of mildewed
biscuits and piss-
like tea that start
up painfully again
his festering ulcer

Still, say no prayer
Spend no tears

for this comrade in
the concrete cage
He has his honour

But for you and I
who daily stroll
under the sun with
fear-locked tongues

You and I who have
doubly pawned
our lives for lies

You and I
who bicker at
the government
yet pay our taxes
rant against
the censor yet
subscribe to the
national newspaper

For you and I, mister
who walk these
city's barren streets
in a midday stupor
save your prayers
and shed your tears
for you and I
walk without honour.

11. The dark side of trees

The truth burns
so they turned
their faces away
from the sun ...

When small liberties
   began to fray ...
When their constitution
   was being chipped away
When their newspapers
   were shut down ...
When their rule of law
   was twisted round ...
When might became right
   and their friends
were carried off screaming
   in the pitch of night ...

They chose silence
feigned blindness
pleaded ignorance.

And now when the shadow
   of the jackboot hangs
ominous over their beloved land
   they walk as zombies
unable to distinguish right from
   wrong from right
their minds furred with lichens
   like the dark side of trees.

The truth burns
so they turned
their faces away
from the sun ...

12. Privileges of the dead

Friends caution: "Take care.
There are dangers everywhere."

Catalogue consequences
of stepping out of line
of speaking out of turn
of going too far
or not going far enough

The deprivations of prison
of solitary confinement
of bread and water
interrogation and torture

So, what to do hence?
Be cowed into silence?

To draw breath in these times
is to walk with danger
only the dead don't have
to look over their shoulder.

13. The animal and insect act

Finally, in order to ensure
absolute national security
they passed the Animal and Insect
Emergency Control and Discipline Act.

Under this new Act, buffaloes
cows and goats were prohibited
from grazing in herds of more
than three. Neither could birds
flock, nor bees swarm ....
This constituted unlawful assembly.

As they had not obtained prior
planning permission, mud-wasps
and swallows were issued with
summary Notices to Quit. Their
homes were declared subversive
extensions to private property.

Monkeys and mynahs were warned
to stop relaying their noisy
morning orisons until an official
Broadcasting Licence was issued
by the appropriate Ministry.
Unmonitored publications and broad-
casts posed the gravest threats
in times of a National Emergency.

Similarly, woodpeckers had
to stop tapping their morse-
code messages from coconut
tree-top to chempaka tree.

All messages were subject
to a thorough pre-scrutiny
by the relevant authorities.

Java sparrows were arrested in
droves for rumour-mongering.
Cats (suspected of conspiracy)
had to be indoors by 9 o'clock
Cicadas and crickets received
notification to turn their amp-
lifiers down. Ducks could not
quack nor turkeys gobble during
restricted hours. Need I say,
all dogs — alsatians, daschunds,
terriers, pointers and even
little chihuahuas — were muzzled.

In the interests of security
penguins and zebras were
ordered to discard their
non-regulation uniforms.
The deer had to surrender
their dangerous antlers.
Tigers and all carnivores
with retracted claws were
sent directly to prison
for concealing lethal weapons.

And by virtue of Article
Four, paragraph 2(b)
sub-subsection sixteen,
under no circumstances
were elephants allowed
to break wind between
the hours of six and six.
Their farts could easily
be interpreted as gunshot.
Might spark off a riot ....

A month after the Act
was properly gazetted
the birds and insects
started migrating south
the animals went north
and an eerie silence
handcuffed the forests.

There was now Total Security.

14. Tocsin

Never say, you do not care
remember, you are
your neighbour's neighbour

and all our destinies
are fanged waves
knit together inextricably

the tide that overtakes
others today, waits
to ambush us tomorrow

alike for each and each
these times, a future unfurls
pencilled with menace
uncertain as the crimpled sea ....

CITIZENS OF THE CONTINENT OF HUNGER

The problem of poverty is nothing new... Almost all societies throughout history had both rich and poor. What is new is the unprecedented increase in the world's wealth, the emergence of affluent nations and their links with the poor societies in a world fast shrinking into a neighbourhood. Besides, the present plight of the poor and certain trends in the affluent societies need to be tackled with apocalyptic urgency.

Good News to the Poor
Published by the World Council
of Churches, Geneva, p. ix

15. Trees

I see
no beauty
in the naked trees
this winter
Their skeletal dignity
is swamped
by images
of Giacometti children
in other places
wire limbs
outstretched
pleading
waiting

The prayer of the trees
will be answered
with flower fruit and leaves
Spring crowns
their waiting

In those other places
of the hoop-eyed children
there is no Spring
only
the waiting

16. Glass

A visit by the Pope to families in two small shacks of
wood and corrugated iron occupied by 10 and
14 people respectively in a squalid, muddy back alley
without sewage was cancelled at the last minute for
unexplained security reasons.

UPI/Reuter

That world will come like a thief
and steal all we possess
Poor and naked, we will be transparent as glass
that both cuts and reflects.

Karol Wojtyla

Nothing else was cancelled

The glittering ceremony
in the Presidential palace
The carefully orchestrated
motorcade across the city

Nothing else was cancelled

The solemn meeting
with the august Cardinal
The Mass for masses
in the majestic cathedral

Nothing else was cancelled

For neither chandelier
nor stained glass
nor pointed mitre
nor rear-view mirror
can cut and reflect
cut and reflect like
the naked and the poor

And their squalid
back alley shacks
their open latrines
their armies of flies
bugs and cockroaches
the sharply pointed
ribs of their children
will ever pose the greater
threat to the security
of thieves who have stolen
their birthright and
rooted themselves in power

The poor have nothing
to lose but their poverty.

17. Statistics

Statistically
it was a rich island
income per capita
one million
per annum

Naturally
it was a shock to hear
half the population
had been carried off
by starvation
Statistically
it was a rich island

A U.N. Delegation
(hurriedly despatched)
discovered however
a smallish island
with a total population
of — 2
Both inhabitants
regrettably
not each a millionaire
as we'd presumed
But one the island owner
Income per annum:
Two million
The other
his cook/chauffeur
shoeshine boy/butler
gardener/retainer
handyman/labourer
field nigger, etc. etc.

The very same
recently remaindered
by malnutrition

Statistically
it was a rich island
Income per capita
per annum
one million

18. Pacifist protest

I have marched down
countless streets
on endless nights
bearing torches
Screamed slogans
at rallies
Chanted poems
in a multitude
of meetings
I have stood
at dozens of
drizzly streetcorners
distributing leaflets
Printed pamphlets
Signed petitions
Picketed
Clenched my fist
and sang
"We shall overcome"
at more embassies
than I care to remember

Yes, I have listened
to the voice of conscience
and duly protested
in a hundred million places

Yesterday, I received this letter
from a friend in a faraway place:

Dear brother, it said, the drought worsens.
For weeks now our family have had no food.
Each of my five children is bloated with
kwashiorkor: their hair lank, the cheeks
swollen. My wife carefully winds her sari
a little tighter around her stomach every
morning in order to lessen the hunger cramps.

She tries to put on a brave face for the sake
of the children. This evening I journeyed
to my mother's cousin to borrow a few
rupees or even a cigarette tin of rice,
but his situation too is critical. How
can I return to the house once more empty-
handed? I cannot bear to look yet again
into my daughter's eyes — wet with disappointment.
There is no choice. May my God forgive me,
but by the time you receive this letter, I
would have put an end to the suffering of my
beloved wife, my five children and myself.
Goodbye brother ....

Do you still believe in non-violence?

19. Morals

Which lover's embrace
under which bower
threatened which nation?
Whose cheongsam-slit
started a war?
Who was felled by a kiss?
Who was hit by a caress?
Was anyone blitzed by a wink?

Which farmer lost his house?
Which soldier lost his eye?
Which river lost its fish?

Talk about immorality
And i will show you
disruptive condominiums
like giant phalluses
thrusting into our sky;
factories like brazen
exhibitionists spouting
their slime into our sea;
i will show you
ruttish bulldozers
debauching virgin forests.

Which Court of Morals
will check the lubricity
of developers and politicians?

Which statute will
cover the pollution
of language and culture?

Who will legislate
against the degradation
of poverty and hunger?

Which Moral Code
will protect our children
from the obscenity of missiles?

Talk about immorality ...

20. The continent of hunger

The Continent of Hunger
has no boundaries
Its Capitals stretch
from Rio to Chicago
Kingston to Addis Ababa
Naples to Calcutta
Jakarta to Buenos Aires

It's children are
of every race
creed and colour
but have no difficulty
in recognizing each other
by their uniform of rags
and their universal birthmarks:
bamboo limbs,
saucer-eyes, pumpkin bellies ...

Each citizen
of this Continent
has a passport
to the Dominion
of Disease
Without let
or hindrance
he may explore
Kwashiorkor
Pellagra
Beri-beri
Cholera
Malaria
Rickets
Scurvy
T.B.

As the Flag of Tears
is lowered each morning
The National Anthem
— a grinding rumble —
can be heard playing
deep in the bowels
of every citizen

The enemies of the Continent
of Hunger are many
Their names are Lonrho, Gulf,
Rothmans Tobacco, Barclays,
Coca Cola, General Motors,
I.T.T. and the United Fruit Co.

Besides having to fight
these Big Businesses
and Multinationals
the citizens of Hunger
have to contend also
with twisted politicians
purblind clergy
corrupt generals
and the fat greasy men
who traffic in human misery

For far longer than China
the peoples of this world
have refused admission
of this Continent
Yet, the Continent of Hunger
did not rise overnight
from the sea
It has been pieced together
over the years
mathematically

with a multitude of stones
quarried from that
monumental rock in men's hearts

Gentlemen, you have the facts
I now demand full
and immediate recognition
of this Continent of Hunger!

21. Portrait of an old lady

A lifetime shuttling
to and from rooms
the size of handkerchiefs.

Fetching and carrying
cooking and scrubbing
shaping the ramshackle

kiosk into a habitable
home for her children
her children's children

never complaining, but
time exacted its toll:
that cang of years

stooped her shoulders;
and decades of pinched
air imploded her

dry weather-polished
face into a diaspora
of pain-scored rivers.

3.5 TONS OF T.N.T.

The arms trade is a new form of intervention,
maintaining and developing dominance-dependence
relationships, and encouraging repression and violation
of human rights. Militarism leads to massive allocation
of human and material resources to research and
production in the military sector in all countries, at the
cost of lowering the priority of meeting the needs of
human development.

We believe that the time has come when the
churches must unequivocally declare that the
production and deployment as well as the use of
nuclear weapons are a crime against humanity and that
such activities must be condemned on ethical and
theological grounds.

Gathered for Life
Published by the World Council
of Churches, Geneva, pp. 75, 137

22. For bloody peace sake

As no man's the aggressor
but everyone's a good neighbour ...

    then why are we taking rice
    out of the mouths of our children
    to arm another battalion?

As no one's territorial
but everybody's neutral ...

    then why are we shelving
    plans to house the poor
    to build a nuclear reactor?

As no one wants hostility
but each man loves tranquillity ...

    then why do we honour more
    doctors of chemical warfare
    than those who cure and care?

And why, why, why
if we're all anti-war
and all for harmony
for bloody peace sake
tell me why is every
body walking around
with bullet-capped teeth
and a hydrogen bomb
under each armpit?

23. Afterwards

After the debates
in the United Nations

After the clarion
of 4-star Generals

After the cannons
fire and mortar

After the CX
napalm and neutron

Jackal and vulture
will hold dominion

After the grand
festival of mushrooms

A phalanx of flies
will inherit this land.

24. Radiation and the rubaiyat

And yes, i too am
tired of protest.
O to be done
with this madness
and like Khayyam
take to the wilderness
with a loaf of bread
a flask of wine
a book of verse
and a wild wild lass ...

But now beneath
that nuclear
bough, Omar
there's no paradise
the bread crumbles
to radio-active pieces
the wine is toxic
the maiden
    leukemic
a skeleton
screaming, not singing
in a wilderness
    of ash.

25. Of war, grass and flowers
(for Chee Ling)

One evening, after the sun
had dropped into that bowl
of blood — we call the sea —
splashing the sky with fire ....

i found myself in our garden
relating to flowers the insanity
of war, the pain and the horror.

In the middle of a story about
a child who had lost her mother,
i heard something softly rustle ....

glancing across my shoulder
i noticed the newly-mown grass
beginning to hackle in terror.

26. Twilight
(for the children of War)

The children
    haunt me most
        at twilight
Twilight
    now turned to
        blood seeping
through
    bandages of cloud
            wrapped tight
round
    the earth's brow
            as another
wounded day
    dies away
        into the night

27. Military two-step

While millions are still in need of basic amenities such
as food, shelter, medicare and education, expenditure
on arms today has escalated to such a point that for
each man, woman and child there is now 3.5 tons of
T.N.T.

You say your shack
needs restoration
the roof leaks
the walls crack
it's a rat and cock-
oach abomination.

Now don't you worry
you can always jive
with your 3.5
tons of T.N.T.

You say the children
are in dire need
of an education
they're bright and eager
but you can't afford
kindergarten or teacher

Now don't you worry
you can always jive
with your 3.5
tons of T.N.T.

You say the family
is always hungry
there's no food
in the larder
and you have to walk
six scorching miles
for a pail of water.

Now don't you worry
you can always jive
with your 3.5
tons of T.N.T.

You say your daughter
died last month
from chronic cholera
she would've been saved
but you couldn't raise
the fees for a doctor

Now don't you worry
   you can always jive
   with your 3.5
   tons of T.N.T.

A POET,
NOT A POSTMAN

Beggars
cockroach our city
Politicians
in their Mercedes
whizz by in luxury

As long
as one man
has no shirt
and his M.P.
has two...
count me out
of any Party!

From *Bones and Feathers* by Cecil Rajendra
Published by Heinemann Educational
Books (Asia) Ltd., p. 79

28. My message

And now you ask
what is my message
i say with Nabokov
i am a poet
not a postman
i have no message.

but i want the cadences
of my verse to crack
the carapace of indifference
prise open torpid eyelids
thick-coated with silver.

i want syllables
that will dance, pirouette
in the fantasies of nymphets
i want vowels that float
into the dreams of old men.

i want my consonants
to project kaleidoscopic visions
on the screens of the blind
and on the eardrums of the deaf
i want pentameters that sing
like ten thousand mandolins.

i want such rhythms
as will shake pine
angsana, oak and meranti
out of their pacific
slumber, uproot them-
selves, hurdle over
buzz-saw and bull-dozer
and rush to crush
with long heavy toes
merchants of defoliants.

i want stanzas
that will put a sten-gun
in the paw of polar-bear and tiger
a harpoon under the fin
of every seal, whale and dolphin
arm them to stem
the massacre of their number.

i want every punctuation —
full-stop, comma and semi-colon
to turn into a grain of barley
millet, maize, wheat or rice
in the mouths of our hungry ;
i want each and every metaphor
to metamorphose into a rooftop
over the heads of our homeless.

i want the assonances
of my songs to put smiles
on the faces of the sick
the destitute and the lonely
pump adrenalin into the veins
of every farmer and worker
the battle-scarred and the weary.

and yes, yes, i want my poems
to leap out from the page
rip off the covers of my books
and march forthrightly to
that sea of somnolent humanity
lay bare the verbs, vowels
syllables, consonants … and say

"These are my sores, my wounds;
this is my distended belly;
here i went ragged and hungry;
in that place i bled, was tortured;
and on this electric cross i died.
Brothers, sisters, HERE I AM."

29. Art for art's sake

Let us rescue poetry
from the barbarians
Those who would reduce
it to a flag, a slogan
a vehicle for propaganda

Let us cleanse poetry
of everything political
of causes, campaigns...
the stock-in-trade
of the crude pamphleteer

Let us return poetry
to the realms
of pure art
resuscitate it with
the essence of nature

Yes, let us give it back
its true noble stature
and enshrine it in
its rightful sanctum
sanctorum of culture

But when the last leaf
quivers to the hot earth
from the last
chemical-riddled tree
and the last grasshopper
limps away into the sun
and the last beleaguered
ant-eater turns halt-
ingly towards the sea
and the last songbird
plummets from its
ash-gloved perch

and the last soldier
twitches in his ditch
and the last oil-slick
moves in to devour
the last of our beaches
who will explain
"Art for art's sake"
to the gasping fishes?

30. To my country

if i did not care
i would not dare
your many imperfections

i would sing
only your praises
picking the best
ignoring the rest

but i am no
starry-eyed lover
i cannot cover
your many blemishes

so if i snarl
at your greed
your subterranean
prejudices ...

the callousness
of your children
your many many
unkindnesses ...

bear with me beloved
love and hate
are forged
in the same cauldron

faults in another
that would not matter
in our loved ones
assume
cataclysmic proportions

one loathes the worst
in those one loves best

and if i did not care
i would not dare
chart
your many imperfections

31. Confessional

For the man (Cecil Rajendra) has talent, which has so
far been squandered. He isn't anywhere near being the
poet he could have been had he been as consistently
exercised by the ideal of poetry as agonizing if also
joyous creation and arduous or even fastidious craft as
much as he has been concerned with poetry as
"sincere", "committed" statement in the cause of
social and humanitarian issues.

Malaysian professor critic

And yes, yes i confess
spendthrift i've squandered
what meagre talent i have
on unpoetic issues like
war and want and refugees.

An arduous task, maybe ...
not joyous but agonizing
and at the end of the day
there is no little bouquet
from windy, ersatz critics.

Spare me your fatuous
condescension, professor;
there's nothing fastidious
about blood or hunger.
Ever tried stopping a tank
with a neatly crafted stanza?

Or, filling a child's belly
with an over-ripe metaphor?
Yes, yes i confess with Owen
i'm exercised by other ideals
my concern has always been
the future of MAN not poetry!

32. No celebratory song

So long
as car-parks take
precedence over hospitals
multi-storeyed hotels
over homes for people
irrelevant factories
over the paddy-fields
of our daily sustenance

I shall
sing no celebratory song
no matter
how many suns go down
This tongue
will be of thistle and thorn
until they right the wrong

So long
as Law comes before Justice
the edifice before service
the payment before treatment
and appearance before essence

I shall sing no celebratory song

So long
as the poet is debased
and the businessman praised
the realist rewarded
and the idealist denigrated

I shall
sing no celebratory song
no matter
how many suns go down

This tongue
will be of thistle and thorn
until they right the wrong

So long
as foreign investors
devastate our estate
and the voice of capital
speaks louder than
the pleas of fishermen

So long
as blind bulldozers
are allowed unchecked
to gouge our landscape
and multinationals
licensed to run
amuck across this land

I shall
sing no celebratory song

So long
as our rivers and streams
our beaches, our air
our oceans and trees
our birds, our fish
our butterflies and bees
are strangled, stifled
polluted, poisoned
crushed, condemned ....
by lop-sided development

I shall
sing no celebratory song
no matter
how many suns go down
This tongue
will be of thistle and thorn
until they right the wrong

33. Song of hope

At that hour
when the sun
slinks off
behind hills
and night
— a panther —
crouches
ready to spring
upon our un-
suspecting city ...

i want to sing
the coiled desires
of this land
the caged dreams
of forgotten men

i want to sing
of all that was
but no longer is
of all that
never was but
could have been

i want to sing
the obsidian
unspelled hopes
of our children
i want to sing
to remind us
never to despair
that every hour
every minute
somewhere on the face
of this earth
it is glorious morning.